BOBWEAVING DETROIT

BOBWEAVING DETROIT

The Selected Poems of
Murray Jackson

EDITED WITH A POSTSCRIPT BY
TED PEARSON AND KATHRYNE V. LINDBERG

WAYNE STATE UNIVERSITY PRESS
DETROIT

African American Life Series
For a complete listing of books in this series please visit our Web site at http://wsupress.wayne.edu

Series Editors:

Melba Joyce Boyd
Department of Africana Studies, Wayne State University

Ron Brown
Department of Political Science, Wayne State University

Copyright © 2004 by Wayne State University Press,
Detroit, Michigan 48201. All rights are reserved. No part of this book
may be reproduced without formal permission.
Manufactured in the United States of America.
08 07 06 05 04   5 4 3 2 1

Thanks to my friends and colleagues for their support, particularly
those who looked at draft after draft and still encouraged me to finish:
Jennie Needleman, Laura Roop, David Victor, and Eugene Haun.
Special thanks to Climetene McClain, Debra Harris, Edna Friedman,
and Teresa Boczar —MJ.

Earlier versions of some of these poems appeared in *Woodland Sketches:
Scenes from Childhood* (X-Press), *Watermelon Rinds & Cherry Pits*
(Broadside Press), and *New Poems From the Third Coast* (Wayne State UP).
The editors have made every effort to identify the publishers of any
uncollected poems included in this volume. They regret any omissions.

Library of Congress Cataloguing-in-Publication Data

Jackson, Murray (Murray E.)
   Bobweaving Detroit : the selected poems of Murray Jackson / edited
with a postscript by Ted Pearson and Kathryne V. Lindberg. — 1st ed.
      p. cm. — (African American life series)
   ISBN 0-8143-3194-7 (pbk. : alk. paper)
   1. African Americans—Poetry. 2. Detroit (Mich.)—Poetry. 3. Blues
(Music)—Poetry. I. Pearson, Ted. II. Lindberg, Kathryne V. III. Title.
IV. Series.
   PS3560.A2553B63 2004
   811'.6—dc22
   2003015787

When the last rattle of defiance
stumbles through the chamber
I fetch the echo

POEMS FOR KATHRYNE

and for
Lawrence Jackson
Christopher David Jackson
Orville Linck

CONTENTS

PAST(ORAL)

AFTER HOURS

FOREWORD

I am pleased to introduce this special edition of *Bobweaving Detroit: The Selected Poems of Murray Jackson*. During our years together at Wayne State University, I was fortunate indeed to have Murray's steadfast friendship and wise counsel.

Murray Jackson gave his intellect to the world and his heart to higher education, especially to Wayne State. He excelled here as a student athlete while earning bachelor's and master's degrees in Humanities, and subsequently was the university's assistant dean of students and assistant to the vice president for urban affairs. He became a member of our Board of Governors and served with distinction until his retirement in 2001.

Murray's was a life of infinite interests, expressed in both his vocations and avocations. His service to higher education included teaching at the University of Michigan, and he was founding president of Wayne County Community College. Murray also was an enthusiastic civil rights activist, a steadfast advocate for youth and first executive director of the Detroit Council of the Arts.

As *Bobweaving Detroit* amply testifies, he also was a poet who deserved the substantial reputation earned through his books and contributions to many publications and anthologies. His poetry courses at Wayne State reflected both his love for people and for the city that was his home.

Murray's poetic voice is in fact a clear, acute echo of the pulse, argot, and ambience of Detroit. Through these pages the city's streets, its open and secret places, the noise and dust and human drama of a great metropolis come to vibrant life. The people we meet here are so real that they often seem to turn from these pages and stare us in the face. *Bobweaving Detroit* is truly an extraordinary glimpse into places that Murray Jackson knew very well—the city, yes, but also the myriad terrains of the human heart.

Irvin D. Reid
President
Wayne State University

STREET-SCARRED AND DIGNIFIED

Sledge's Barber Shop

Mr. Clay Sledge from Tombigbee, Alabama,
just two cheeks of tobacco juice from the Mississippi,
had three chins, working on number four.

You could tell that few servings of
hot brown corn bread, chitlins, greens
and neck bones got past Clay Sledge.

The shop was clean, spittoons polished most of the time.
When me and my brother went to the barber shop,
Mr. Sledge needed no instructions. Cue-balled again.

You could get your hair cut, and your shoes shined
sometimes. If we listened hard,
we could hear a story or two about girls

and things we did not understand.
But the men laughed, slapped their knees
and made funny noises.

You know what they call 'the world's
oldest profession'? It ain't true.
It's men lying to each other in barber shops.

Things Ain't What They Used To Be

Telling lies older than us, Billy Lamplighter
stands on the steps of the middle court,
watches cars and people, thinks of days
when he danced on a forehead or two.
He could dance, Billy thought and smiled.

Geechee George, slick black hair, pimp shoes,
a bottle of Jump Steady clutched in his hand,
swings and kicks at a brown-spotted dog,
Old Pots, the neighborhood pet.

Billy saw Geechee, called him,
"Why you messin' with the dog for?"
Geechee grinned, "Cause I wanna, why?
How much you weigh, man?"

Billy stepped back, click-popped his blade,
"Five hundred pounds on your collar, motha."
Geechee's face got heart-attack serious.
"I don' wanna see you on the block.
If I do, I'll be on your ass like white on rice."

Popping sweat faster than a foundry worker,
half-looking at Billy. "Yeah, Billy, okay.
All I did was kick the dog."
Billy looked at his blade.
"You got one last time to do that."

Eight Ball, Side Pocket

Soft side of Hastings, Oakland Avenue,
Wilfred's Billiard Parlor jammed between
The Pig Bar-B-Q and the Echo Theatre.

Slick Herman chalks his cue with resolution,
blue powder whispers to the floor.
He misses an easy bank-shot in the corner.

Safe Eddie would always leave you on the rail
or hidin' behind balls you didn't want to shoot.
And steady Jerome looks for non-believers.
Hasn't missed a bank-shot in four days.

Silent Ambrose shoots nine-ball
with Ralph, the Merchant.
Ralph accuses Ambrose of moving his balls
for a better angle; calls Silent a name.

Silent flashes quicker-than-light
two inches of switchblade to Merchant's jugular.
In the stop-stillness of the moment,
you could hear a rat piss on cotton.
"Don't you call me that, ever."

Silent wins by forfeit. Merchant can't
find a cue that will sit still in his hand.

Northend

Terrence Willaby hustled beer and pop bottles
for deposit at the corner store,
collected pounds of paper and metal for the junkyard
to help him make it on his stale gravy sandwiches
and pay for his sometime radiator heat.

The boys on the corner didn't like Terrence;
that was no name for a real man anyway.
Willaby scrounged up a dime buried in street garbage,
stooped to pick it up, saw a number
on the back of a truck, played the number.

That night Willaby's number came out.
He huckle-bucked the alley countin' his money.
Big Bad Tampa Red squeaked next to the apartment,
"Willaby, gimme some money." Willaby looked
at Red, smiled. "I ain't givin' you shit."

Kept on countin' and steppin', countin' and steppin'.
Next day, *Countin'* Terrence Willaby.

Georgia Brown

Sliding the south side, she skipped rope
to the beat rhythm of the streets.
Hyde Park, Kenwood, Woodlawn,
Roosevelt; Loyola schooled her needs.

Georgia stared down a long brown table
made strong in the Mandingo rain forest,
embossed with purple Watusi seals,
pierced with slivers of oak bark from Carolina,
oiled and polished bright.

Gravel-voiced, tongue-scarred Georgia,
trapped in the crazy glue of winter,
walked on streets of ice and snow
with cracked hands, burning ears.
Never a "can't do"—just a "give me time, I will."

Georgia saw broken eyes
that could only gawk, empty stomachs,
landlords with notices to quit,
utilities next to go.

Stubborn. Headstrong
like the wind that jitterbugs
down Michigan Avenue,
taking names and kicking ass.

Only once did I see the hurt
of betrayal in her eyes: the City's plan
for the homeless, a greedy deception,
new wounds stitched over old.

Georgia went back to the table,
looked again. "Don't call me 'sweet.'
My name is Georgia."

I Got It

On plain old black asphalt,
white bonneted, broad-brimmed
ribbons the color of royalty,
pushcart all dressed up,
rainbow sheets, big sign
red and white
                    I GOT IT

Street gypsy selling his wares:
skillets, pots, an almost-cashmere
sweater (crooked label from Saks),
bent bicycle wheel shining
like a new dime, a real pearl
necklace, zircon-diamond rings
from the Five-and-Ten,

six rolls of Louis XIV wallpaper,
two bottles—Nature Boy,
Cadillac Club—one half-empty,
one half-full. Out the side
of his mouth: "If I ain't got it today,
I'll have it tomorrow. Tell me
what you need. I got it."

Corner Gossip

Velma stood tall and foxy on the corner
across from the Cellar Door.
Regina, street-scarred and dignified,
oiled to her own good uses.
Sally Ann, with her black net stockings,
filled every twist of silk with her fine stems.
Early Alphonso had a room upstairs.

Regina and Sally modeled, strained,
watched, and hooked. Velma was new
to the sidewalk and needed help.
Early fetched, carried food and drink,
anything to help turn a trick.

When the sun sucked up the shade
of Brush Street, Early's compensation
depended on who was tired.
After the shift, Velma was available.
This particular day, Early came late.
Velma was upset. Early wasn't.

Ten No-Trump

Wrinkled lips curled, Mellow Man
just smiled. He called them all rookies.
The invention of bragging rights—September '38.
310 East Canfield, Apartment 6.

Papa Steele, proprietor: a good bridge player,
not as good as he thought, but alright.

He woofed loud and long about his bridge game,
puffing on his two-for-a-nickel John Ruskin cigar,
shouting at Mellow Man for having a piano-hand
that needed little skill.

Vic from the Islands: black straight hair, darting eyes.
If you've seen Peter Lorre, that was Vic,
good technician at the table.
Nobody messed with him; he could play.

Trussed up in his undertaker's collar,
Ira, big as a box of toothpicks, a handful of safety matches,
quiet, thoughtful, decent enough.
Now that I think of it, he reminded me of Cassius.

Cliff thought he knew bridge as good as Goren,
who lived across the hall. Whenever Cliff talked about bridge,
it was war. His only rival, the neighbor next door.

Henry and Dot could finesse oil
to the bottom of a water glass.
Dot was the first woman in the bragging club
and the best player in the house.

Nick Harris, sometime player,
spent his days at the Ford foundry, lost an arm
stamping out Mr. Henry's metal.

On special occasions, me and my brother
were allowed to play with the big boys.
When we played well, we were sent on errands
to the grocery store, or to take Bogie,
the big black-and-orange Doberman, for a walk.

We learned how to play anyway.

No Game Today

Dressed in patent-leather brimmed
caps and store-bought bow ties,
Felix and Smitty owned City Cab 977.
Felix worked days; Smitty the nights.

Smitty lived at 291 Canfield,
Apartment 6, right over home plate.
Felix lived wherever he could.

As the two old friends polished
the yellow and red coat-of-arms on the door
of 977, they reminisced: Mr. Whiteside
was due ten dollars on the Packard

pickup truck, so Smitty and Felix left
Turtle Neck in a slow hurry. The pickup
stopped whenever it got tired.

They took fares to the white picket fences
of Grosse Pointe—lawns cut evenly,
all in order, the way it's supposed to be.
Then downtown, Paradise Valley—

the Cotton Club, the Three Sixes, The Flame
Show Bar—sometimes all the way to
Michigan Central Railroad; then maybe
Six Mile and Woodward, the sticks.

The day shift done, the meter pushed
for the last time, Smitty parked on home plate.
Some days, he would park in the alley,
watch us play, laugh, and cheer us on.

Smitty's kids, Big Old George and
Horace, couldn't play a lick.
Ambrose and Micky didn't even care.

Sometimes we had to let Phyllis play;
she was good as the big boys.
Humped-up black backsides pressed
against the coal-chute door.

Shining in the sunlight, City Cab 977.
No game today.

Gifts

I.

I stood in the tunnel warehouse
holding hands with my brother and Dad,
with our Red Flyer wagon that the Goodfellows left.
We came for potatoes, salt pork, beans, and flour.
The lines were long, but we had to stay. Strangers
waited with us, against the flush of winter.

II.

Lunch at the Book Cadillac, second basement.
Our uncle worked in the Kay Danzer Flower Shop.
He took roses to the stadium ticket window.
We got to see the Tigers play the Yankees.
Greenberg hit one out onto Cherry Street.

III.

I had a report due in Social Science.
Finished it while Mom did the dishes.
I washed my safety-patrol belt every Monday.
Mr. Loving expected them to be spotless.
I brushed, scrubbed, and soaked it.
Mom suggested table salt. It glowed.

IV.

Mom told Dad I wanted to go to college.
We didn't have money for school.
Dad pulled out the blue pin-striped suit
that he saved for special good times,
looked it over, fondled the jacket, took the suit
to Lewis's, the pawnshop on Gratiot.

Johnny B.

Johnny seemed to be two deep breaths from the joint—
some friends had been in and out,
ready to go again.
Johnny punched out cut-glass streets;
they punched him too.

Louie da Hood, Quiet Sam,
Chicki Sherman, Westside Jim.
Tuxedo Street in Highland Park.
His mother always invited us to tea,
red beans and gravy.

More friends worked at the Cavalier Club,
Baccarat, Barboot, some 21.
Anything else, small action.
Corky, Bucko, Mac Parshea,
were the entry and exit men at the Cavalier.

Sometimes they rode bare-knuckle
for the shark school.
Skilled in the art of persuasion.
Two plus two was not four.
Two plus two was four plus ten percent.

One afternoon, Johnny wanted to go to college.
Came to visit me with Jake, his main man.
Good students, eager to know.
Assigned as their advisor, guess I was
responsible for some of their learning.

One day during class break—
fifth race, Hazel Park, serious study,
daily racing form, tip sheet—
Johnny interrupted his tense research
to ask me a question about Egyptian art.

We all needed to get out.
Stunned momentarily, I responded
"First things first.
The winner in the fifth.
Then, maybe Egyptian art."

Baby Ray

Baby Ray cribbed on the black-topped
streets, scratched high honors

at Southeastern; his folks left
for Vegas to make it big.

He always hummed
"Someone To Watch Over Me"

Won't you tell her please
to put on some speed?

We used to call him Mooch 'cause
he was always on empty. Not anymore.

Raymond found the fast lane.
His street cabinet helped.

Wolf, the con man for all seasons,
Fast-Break Benjamin, always in foul trouble,

Bee, her dime-sized waist and healthy hips,
Stu, the police advisor,
and Phil, the soothsayer of John R.

Early mornings at Pindilly's to play "21."
If the cards fell right,

all the hustlers in the joint got gappers.
A fresh start tomorrow.

Then the Cakewalk to the Frolic
where Arnett Cobb was working out.

The Garfield Lounge for chicken in a basket
and on to Sassy Sarah at the Flame.

Sam

A phone call from Sam before 11 p.m.
didn't count. He knew every name
in Detroit—some in Lansing, too.
And those he didn't know, you didn't.

Who was this man, bent like a weed
wafting in the wind,
with soft slick eyes that burned
flush with a constant need to know?

The President speaks for the University.
Sam spoke to him.

Sam allowed us to indulge his passion.
His credentials got him into meetings.
Less trouble in than out, he bojocked
secretaries, deans, and other keepers.

He knew the power of selective memory.
Informed words could be costly.
From the hard granite perch of his roaring
solitude, he knew us all.

Growing Up Colored

The Old Boy walks from Canfield and Woodward
to Mansfield, Highland Park Ford Plant,
with Herman Davis and Sam Rustin, looking
to find Mr. Henry's man, Marshall,
who could say these boys are alright.

Pickup men take your number and duck
between alleys and houses, not to get caught.
If you hit, you hope he'll hop to your door
with the money.

Trying to be the temporary weather-boy,
you look at the sky, scratch your head,
dig in your ass, shuffle at the same time,
waffling through a minefield of eggshells.
You got rhythm.

Jabberwocking through the pains of being colored.
Dancing sometimes, even jitterbugging
through a Strauss waltz. Friday night, rent party.
Eva's again? After, we could get to the fish fry
at Wimpy's. Up all Saturday night.

Pray a little on Sunday. Stand on tiptoes,
straining to peer on the other side of death, singing
the edges of despair—"Swing Low, Sweet Chariot."
Monday, start to be colored again.

Detroit Addendum—*for Philip Levine*

Not Virgil, not Beatrice.
You, Philip, took us on slick city streets
to the pimped belch of Detroit

DODGE MAIN WYNADOTTE CHEMICAL FORD ROUGE CHEVROLET GEAR & AXLE
in one unbroken line.

Riverrun past burning moat, round
sanguine cauldrons, ending and beginning over again
in a coke-oven shake-out.

From fiery epicenters, black faces,
white faces, glow red. *We stare* through words
into fire until our *eyes are also fire.*

Things passed from hand to hand in darkness
that we, like machines, cannot see.

King Henry's table, seating in split shifts,
neck bones 'n' ribs, corned beef on rye
with mustard, kielbasa and raw onions.

Philip, I do remember a black man,
the Old Boy who danced all night
at Ford Highland Park—my father.

What Work Is is work.

PHOTO SHADOWS

Pigeon-Toed Knock-Kneed

Going with the pitch from first to third
on an infield hit, molasses rolling over pancakes.

Flatbush, Ebbets Field, the real Dodgers—
Erskine, Campanella, PeeWee, Newcombe, Hodges.

When the Giants' pitcher attempts to rearrange
his rib cage and give him double vision,

Jackie drops a soft bunt down the first-base line,
seducing the pitcher to field the ball

while Jackie rips through him toward the bag.
He always came ready to play.

You sensed the rage building from Alabama,
UCLA, the Army, Montreal, to all the playing fields,

and now the Dodgers—being spat on, cursed
and niggered at. He came to play, and did.

Opening Day at Ebbets, pumped up, inflamed,
waiting for the ump to give the word.

First the anthem. In his private space, his blue cap
over his heart, it was worth the wounds.
The land of the brave and the home of the free.

Ebbets Field is gone now, no place to reminisce,
but his name is carved on base paths

in Yankee Stadium, Wrigley Field, Forbes Field,
and a place called Cooperstown.

What do we owe Jackie Robinson?
To remember the struggle against the current
is not to ask—but to demand.

The Old Mongoose—*for Mac*

Archwald Lee Wright, born age three,
bobweaved himself into Archie Moore,
roamed the backsides of Union Street
where guards watched for ride robbers.

Stole streetcar change in order to eat,
did time in reform school. Learned
to protect himself with his hands
so he wouldn't have to be reformed.

Archie knew early, before his first fight
with Piano Mover Jones, that it would take
more than taut skin over angry muscle
to punch holes in the heavy bag.

He moved with flashes of light, throwing
hooks and jabs that jarred eardrums.
Always thinking, he finessed opponents.

Outdoors, he forced them to face the sun,
stepped on their toes to keep them from moving.
Stared Carl "Bobo" Olson down in three.

Archie laughed. With his magic diet—
grapefruit, sauerkraut juice and beef:
chew the beef, suck the juice, spit out
the rest—he outlived eight managers.

San Diego Goodbye—*1944, Jacksaw Arena*

Oxhead McIntosh, out of White Plains,
could hit hard. I was quicker.
He was always talkin', "Nigger boy,
where'd you get those funny green eyes?
You know you ain't supposed to win."

I couldn't keep my mind on the fight.
"Black boy, I'm beatin' your ass."

He dropped his right to hammer me
with his left. I slipped the punch
and landed a left hook to the jaw.
His jaw dropped, splintered, hung
like a door with a missing hinge.

He clutched and fell, whirled
upright, then dropped, pawing his jaw
to push the hurt away.

I stood in the corner, ready
to break his face again. Then
I saw his eyes—panicked, hurt, lost.
Blood trickled from his lips
and splattered the canvas.

I climbed through the ropes for the last time.

Shore Leave 1945

Rufus Muleshoe, Chicago Gump, Prentis and me
in our dress blues on John R.
We looked for the Pelican, fine baked chicken.
All we needed was our Southern Comfort
so we could swagger in Motown.

Woodward Avenue, Sanders Vanilla Confectionery,
streetcars running on rails.
Ten cents would take you to the river,
a zipped-up view of Canada,
then north to the State Fairgrounds.

Downtown, Hudson's and Crowley's
toe to toe on the other side of the Library.
At the Fox Theatre, me and Prentis stood
on seats, bouncing to Benny and Bags.

Everybody who was anybody
met at Kern's Clock.

Hastings Street pawnshops, Zimmerman's
always ready to help you get over.
Ladies in waiting who wanted you
to have two dollars' worth of fun.
No-name businesses with anything you need.

The Willis and Mayfair theaters
housed your dreams for half a night.
Barthwell's pumped-up ice-cream factory,
Stefanski's Deli, thick slices of
hot corned beef, a real dill pickle.

Neisner's Five-and-Dime, the Cozy Corner
where Muleshoe tells lies and slow-drinks beer.
Green's Bar-B-Q, Sam's Cut-Rate—
what you bought from Sam
didn't wear well in the rain.

Store-front houses, between stores, on top of stores.
Brown and gray rats stalked under rotten
floorboards covered with shiny linoleum.
Roaches moved to the beat in the dark.

A shot-glass from the Frolic Show Bar.
Sonny Wilson's sleeping place, a dollar a night.
Chicago Gump, slicker than Vaseline,
always put his money in the pillow.

We followed his move.

Pierre Toussaint

I.

Stubborn feet touch white sand
with calloused toes, purpled from
the heat of Africa. Back and arms
corded like Calypso trees.

Caribbean sun makes heavy harvest,
calls the slavehands to strip the cane
and make the master rich.

On white sand, rippled with blood,
Slaves stand and stretch their backs,
hard against the lash.

Pierre hears the loud pounding,
holds out his hands,
fastens his belt, comes to serve.

II.

The indifferent cool of North America
like a sharp machete-nick fires memories:
blue bubble of Caribbean sky, purple bougainvilleas,
orange mimosa pushing humid air.

Pierre Toussaint (his master, John Bernard)
came to the East River docks. Saw
the gutted ruins from the great fire. Heard
the echoes of revolution, New York

harbor pounded with shell and musket
where other men died for freedom.
Pierre mended the bloody skin of slaves,
pushed broken bones and muscle together.

Maiden Lane boarded up against the fever.
"Go to Toussaint; he will help. He knows what to do."
Like a soft Creole whisper, Pierre crossed
the barricades, saw jaundiced eyes and skin,

heard the pounding of wood on flesh.

III.

Fifty years of Mondays on cobblestone at St. Peter's,
outstretched hands seeking alms for
a school for girls, a place for homeless children.

Pierre still brought food to Master's widow,
changed to a high-collared shirt under
gold and red waistcoat to serve her dinner.

He was no traitor to emancipation. The staff
in him measured the rod. Freedom deferred,
he purchased the liberty of slaves. Freer than
the master, he required no manumission.

Light shadows the slab marked "Pierre"

Chapel Street and West Broadway, hidden
in a corner, on a corner, by gray brick walls
fenced with begonias, a big maple, and two
white rosebushes tucked under a hazy sky.

Pierre could stand the pounding of nails.

Trowbridge School

The cross-town streetcar jugged jogged
down twisting track going east.
On the corner, Matthews Drugs,
Dr. Murphy's office upstairs.
Charles Young Post, nose-to-nose with
Forest Cleaners, then the red-white A & P.

Trowbridge School, pale brick, 1882.

With folded arms and thick heavy hands,
His voice soft and clear, Mr. Pearl
overwatched the right of passage
in the halls—asked me to bring mom
to talk about my playing.

Mom knew the route well, took all
the shortcuts, same as us. Down to Garfield,
Plymouth Church, the vacant lot
our playing field, full of rocks, glass,
everything nobody wanted. Past Federal Truck,
the big tree that grabbed us.

Betty Cain, the girls' gym teacher, always smiled
and seemed to know when to hold our hands.
She took time to talk when we needed talk.
She even taught me to social-dance.

Bill Loving played baseball with the patrol boys
after school. When we finished, he would
show us pictures of him and his brother, Al,
when they were students at Kalamazoo.

Miss Downing had a neat bun of gray-white hair
and a strap as wide as the blackboard chalk-well.
My brother Larry had no trouble in her class.

I spent my time in Miss Cain's home-room,
she of the soft brown skin and
dimpled cheeks. We learned good in her class.
She stood for no messin' around.

Maybe because I was older, the teachers
would ask why I wasn't more like my brother.
What they didn't know was all I ever wanted
was to go with the crack of the bat, turn my
my back to the infield, and catch dreams.

Ladies of Josaphat

They walked the mortared brick of St. Antoine,
high-top shoes laced all the way up,
onto Beaubien where the streetcar ran.
With beads and crosses, they lock-stepped

from the red sandstone chapel of St. Josaphat,
past the three copper-colored iron balls
of the pawnshop, down to our block,
across Brush to John R.

It was whispered around that they were
witches and gypsies from the old country.
I didn't know any better.
Struck dumb, I just watched them.

Celled in their brown and white habits,
their dark vanilla faces smuggled out
smiles as they walked past us.

In the gait of their steps, I thought I heard
an old spiritual, remembered from
a sanctified store-front church on Forest.

> *Yes, I beat the devil runnin'*
> *and I'm on my way to heaven*
> *and the world can't do me no harm.*

Miss Lucy

Squash-yellow scraps of paper,
crumpled, twisted, folded neat.
Picture albums from before Kodak:
outdated dresses and hats.

Cleans pots, pans, and dishes.
Makes roast beef and rolls
with the skill of a surgeon.

Ten dollars on the dresser
for anyone who needs it.

Gnarled, careworn hands glide
over washboards; iron fine shirts,
skirts, slips; move hot things
in and out of stoves,

dust-mop the white folks so
they'll be presentable to each other.

Shoes overrun, feet out, squeak
her workaday rhythms.

Two nephews. Playboy
with his Stetson and pimp shoes,
stands pat on the corner,

twirling his key chain,
looking for action—
and Sam, Great Lakes Steel,

six children and Louise,
hides out in the Bicycle blues,
hoping to learn Georgia Skin.

Sweet Lucy, a one-line obit:
Apartment 109.

Lee

Hanging fire from her lips,
at Cass and Warren, coffee and talk,
a smile that knew before you knew,
hacking laughter, tall and straight,
black hair cropped short,
dark eyes that never shut off.

She pricked my hand with
Gammer Gurton's needle, told me
about Beowulf, deep in the bog,
looking for Grendl, the big-headed
monster and his vengeful mama.

Lee, I will rehearse your memory
when the breath of summer pushes
young leaves and sweet vapors,
and when damp scholars with
the quick hands of impatient lovers
revisit Shakespeare's place.

Then I will think of Edmund's
Faerie Queen with her Red Cross Knight,
Robert Greene with three *e's*,
the lusty days of winter on the corner
of Collingwood and Hamilton,
waiting for the bus to campus.

The small, tidy, in-between days
when you and Chet would help us
resurrect a thought or two
with your Old Taylor and our water,
now ambushed by swift-footed time.
I touch books and other things you left.

Robert Brown Elliott

How my voice excites the morning
as I thunder in the halls of Congress.
The dark-eyed stare that is mine alone
stops motion when I fight for South Carolina.

As I listen to the gentleman from Sumter,
I should be derelict in my identity
if I remain in my seat.
I know I frustrate nerves.

Me, Robert Brown Elliott, indentured to none.
Honors—Eton; Law—the King's Council.
My bloodline runs through the Indies;
my place of birth, Boston.

They will honor and respect me
because I am more than equal
to any of them on any occasion.
If only if I would be less uppity.

It was the Irish—men from swamps and bogs—
responsible for the change in suffrage.

I am not Othello, disenchanted
by imperfection, or the black-faced
minstrel who sings, bows, dances.
I am none of these.

I squat, reckoning the blue-eyed sky
outraged by its own infidelity.
In search of old victims for new atrocities
in the name of some god colored white.

My disabilities do not allow me
to be corrupted by the corruption
of others; my vision is not deformed.
Yet I am all of these.

Different times, different places,
but I alone decide when and where.
I may be between dreams.
When between dreams, choices are few.

Dudley Randall

In Paradise Valley, your man Caruso
flashes his ruby stick-pin, stands on
his chair, talks about being colored.

Prophet Jones sashays to his temple
on Hague, floats to the pulpit in ermine
robes, hands outstretched for alms.

Casablanca shadows Orchestra Place,
touts his basement palace, a spot
to look at cards and have a taste.

You catch the mellow harmony of
their beat—siphon time and bottle it,
uncork and stick it in our eye.

Raymond

He rocked back and forth on the soles
of his bitter-brown suede Edmond Clapps,
profiling his lime-sherbert silk pants
so the cuffs barely broke his shoe tops.
He stuttered one day across Woodward,
rummaged around Wayne University, took
a course or two—turned on by law school—
thought he'd be the Clarence Darrow of Detroit.

Some of his main people got busted: Felice
for showing in front of the Chesterfield Show Bar;
Amos Amos with two boxes of white-on-white
French cuffs that didn't belong to him; then
Pigeon-Drop Winslow dropped on The Man
in the Commonwealth Bank one day.

Law School slipped away for a midnight blue
cashmere overcoat and a two-tone hog.
He would dream Istanbul to see a turkey fight,
rain-checked Istanbul for the Olympia
to watch Sugar Ray dispatch pretenders.

Raymond strode back to the streets,
stopped at the Frolic to rack 'em back one time
so they'd remember, then retreated
to his Bamboo Room for a soft taste or two.
He never stopped his jab.

Willie Green

Sharper than a rat turd in July,
he stood on the corner
in his red checkerboard coat,
white flannel pants, and suede
shoes, Thom McCan's best.

Willie was clean.

Tyrone, the town crier, was about to ask
where he copped them fine threads,
but after checkin' the scene,
he just couldn't look at Willie
and that coat at the same time.

Tyrone knew, like Hawkshaw
and Lime Juice, if they didn't tell Willie
he was sharp, they hadda beat his ass.
That day, Willie had the corner to himself.

Firstborn

We walk down a row of steps
braced with ribboned
bundles of orchids and roses.

The breeze, not soft, but kind
enough not to ripple the pond or
bend the trees to distraction,

while yellowjackets disrupt
the rhythm of words
searching the air for sweet smells.

I hold Llenda's hand as Father
Thomas asks me to
place her hand in Michael's.

My hand stutters, then stops.
The second time, I move
her hand from mine to his.

Play Through

18 was a tough hole.
Mac tried to play it tight like a Shubert
quartet. Fronting him, the palace guard:
two ever-shedding evergreens.

He hooked his tee shot a little.
Down the fairway, looking in the rough
for his ball, he walked past tall weeds
and shallow troughs of rain water,
still playing through.

He found his ball almost buried under
thick grass—not a bad lie, even in the rough—then
took his six-iron, feet firm, hands extended.

The ball erupted from the divot like a bird
rifling to the moon, floated to the green,
pin high, and dropped toward the cup with
the hush of a stage whisper, almost a gimme.

PAST(ORAL)

Ars Poetica

With no apologies to Plato
or Marianne Moore, I do like poetry.

To discover whether
the universe swings
from the left or the right
can be hot stuff.

I covet the curve of new words
that wrack the marrow. Do I need
a half-page footnote in foreign
tongues to tell me why?

You'd think some journal sociological
would be the place to discover
why prostitutes prostitute and
hungry mothers are malnourished.

But shadows come from real images, and
I need to know the color and feel of shadows.
If the poet is true and real,
I will inhale the image.

I don't want to listen to Beethoven
and translate what I hear
through EEG scribblings
that meter time.

I must feel color, vitality of movement,
and the force of sound through ears and eyes.
I carve new words from old
to touch the bone of meaning.

I don't need a computer printout
to tell me what I've heard and seen.
I need the rhythm of poetry
that razors language to the quick.

K V L

Spitting fire-hot pieces of light,
she suffers no shade,
reels on the edge of mosaic shards
in search of herself,
forging indelible shadows.

Our slip-cover togas ripped off,
we are naked to ourselves
in circles of square knots,
stalking hermit eyes hidden
in the navel of Tiresias.

Bellowed sounds slap and twist air.
Sun-stoked coals wait in heat,
push to light the prism.
Kathryne gives her hand to dance
soft, to take, touch, tight.

First Class

Our thoughts huddled to ourselves,
I didn't know what to expect—
was I good enough to be there?

We stood around in the hall
memorizing our names outside his room
in a corner of Old Main.

When the door opened, a small neat bunch
of uncomfortable chairs waited.
A grand blackboard with chalk and two erasers.

In one corner, a desk piled with books
and papers, unorganized, stacked together.
Western Civ—History 110.

A small man stood in the middle:
iron-rimmed glasses, a suit
pressed accordion-style.

Dr. Sydney Glazer greeted us, took attendance.
Called each student Mister or Miss.
Me? Mister? What a nice ring.

On the sleeves of his jacket, marks of the trade
as he punched ideas on the blackboard.
His cigarette ash hung like a squirrel's tail.

Professor Glazer always found a way
to round my answers into some kind of sense.
He knew how to make me think I was smart.

We saw Hannibal cross the Alps, Caesar in the Forum,
even glimpsed Herodotus taking notes, and heard
Voltaire: "I don't believe a word you're saying, but . . ."

He counseled me on my chances with the Dodgers,
talked about my mom and my two brothers, called
to congratulate me on my first faculty appointment.

He called me Mister. I called him Dr. Glazer.
Chalk dust on the cuff of his soul.
First class.   First class.

Teach Africa—*for Asa Hilliard*

The dark light of Africa
kissed Cleopatra

long before Caesar and Antony
came to her in their white
togas veined with purple.

Africa, like a hard wind, rages
and caresses with one mighty stroke.
Tell it. What was there? Did one
great hand scoop us together?

Clan to clan, kin to kin,
village to village, we know
no single tradition

Can't you hear the heft
of a thousand songs
splitting the wind to be free?

I, too, hear Africa in America.
A song, syncopated—transposed.

Past(oral)

Breaking bread with dawn, the morning sun
peeled the orange sky bright yellow.

Thatch-roofed shed stashed in a corner
with runaway trees and weeds. Morning glories
bubbled and peeked through the cracks.

Only the flow of oil disturbed the stillness
of blackmen and redmen warring.
Mr. Shaw, the best player on the block,
crowned kings with quick flick.

Freddie, splattered with oil, played now and then
when he wasn't knuckle-deep in a tray of grease.
Freddie fixed cars, if only to fix them again.

George Washington, his hanging shoulder
ripped in a machine at Kelsey-Hayes, played
whenever his medication, "won't let you go"
and "nice and easy," didn't twist him around.

Bill Kegler, man in charge, hopped with his
humped-up foot, watched, and when the time
was right, took a taste with Dad and the boys.

Catch

We start throwing.

Me, with great follow-through,
fingers extended just like I used to
when I was almost with the Dodgers.

I can play catch any time. "Dad, when
was the last time you played catch?"

I could throw a fastball through
the side of a barn door and, with a wrist
like a rubber band, a curveball

that rolled off the edge of a table.
But that was fifty years ago.

I remember the 18-yard touchdown run
that gains ten yards a year.

I sometimes think I still hide in the steam
of the locker room. The Dodgers
were real—and the touchdown.

My grandson Christopher says,
"Granpaw Murray, throw me the ball.

I can play catch."

Jogging Sherwood Forest

No band of merry men: that was yesterday.
Just cars, people, trees, dancing
pieces of light that shimmy through treetops
on sidewalks, rooves, and me.

Bluejays slap the face of air and wheel
like ballerinas, doing their thing, looking
for cloud cover, contemplating worms.

Long-legged blackbirds mimic sea-hawks,
cardinals show their colors,
street-smart pigeons move when they're ready.

Wet streets cultivate tree monsters
that leap from the underworld.

Breaking tracks of snow on Sunday morning
to the Northwest territory—
Eight Mile and Canterbury.

Discarded crumbs from lovers' banquets,
The Colonel and Big Mac feed the birds,
squirrels, and raccoons, even.

No Sheriff of Nottingham.
Just plain old cops.

Tale of the Dinosaur

I.

The EMS blinks orange and red
as it wheezes by stoplights, people, and cars.
Not saving time, just pressing it together.
We stop, charade ourselves into thinking
we have suffocated every tick of borrowed time.
A fistful of air, snatched from the wind,
oozes through fingers that heal.

II.

Time gives us dust from the Acropolis,
mummified spiderwebs in the pyramids.
Time past, folded in wrinkles of earth,
robed in red, shadowboxes in gray trunks,
then sits and waits to be rediscovered.

III.

Indentured to space and the radius
of a compass, time is the only freedom
in the universe. Self-syncopated, it makes
no decisions, just changes lightbulbs
as the crow flies on the tail of the dinosaur.

Detroit–Chicago Train Time

Michigan Central Railroad station,
Doric columns, Corinthian cloisters. Had they voices,
the walls and floors could sing.

World War II troop trains from all over the country
stopped for a moment at Michigan Central.

Now the space from station to train yard
resembles Frankfurt, 1944. Twisted pieces
of concrete and steel like black and red licorice.

Houses that sit and look at you through dirty windows.
Yards back and front littered with cots, chairs, ovens,
refrigerators and, yes, portable swimming pools.

Fields of corn, some cabbage, cows slapping air
in search of flies, horses ogling grass.
19th-century stations: Niles, Kalamazoo, Jackson.

My friend and colleague, Clio, working her con,
a treatise "On Junk," might find this route
the ideal museum for everything nobody wants.

Are You Running With Me?—*for Malcolm Boyd*

Stored in hooded sanctuaries
where you huddle in robes,
clutching candles and
mouthing the mystery.

Sue, deep in your belly,
you ache from wall to wall,
cuddle men with stories
to tell, secrets to hide.

Running rank with residue
from a two-minute lover.
Air like a septic tank.
Come run with me, Jesus.

Down on the corner.
Do you live here?
Smell the shit-filled halls.
Flying roaches and bedbugs jump
beds to chairs and floors.

Hugs, then kisses that touch away
trickles of snot.
The girl-mother with her baby
cradled in squalor.

Are you running with me? Are you?

To My Brother Larry

We giggled and watched
the toes of the world
from our basement window.

Archibald, the music teacher,
peteeting down John R.

Goatmilk Smith made all the rounds,
selling milk to those who wanted it.

Bubbuh was training to be a Sumo,
but he had ingrown bunions and could
be disarmed with a touch of the toe.

Speedy, the pickup man,
made the rounds on Canfield.

He could get numbers in quicker
than Jesse Owens when he outraced
horses at the Fairgrounds.

Lucky, with his stitched-up wagon,
sold twenty-five-pound blocks of ice.

And before school, the clip-clop of
the milkman's horse-cart jarred the street.

When snowflakes crowded the sidewalk,
the courtyard needed shoveling, too.

We rushed from one end to the other, hoping
when we finished that the snow would stop
so we wouldn't have to do it again.

Mom would let us know, or Dad
when he got home from work.

Kroegers on John R had fresh-ground
Country Club coffee. And across the street,
C.F. Smith punched the street
with the smell of just-picked vegetables.

Little Johnnie's never closed—
Mary and Johnnie slept standing up.

We had credit with Firestone.

Saturdays, we vacuumed the halls,
cleaned out the incinerators,
washed the windows in the vestibule.

Dad helped shovel coal in the furnace
to keep the tenants from rattling the pipes.

Night Field

In 1812 and 1823, John Field visited Moscow
and was well received. His music, with that of Hummel
and Rossini, was spoken of as "the rage" in St. Petersburg.
Between 1824 and 1828, he settled in Moscow.

———————

His shadow, an afterthought, specters
the pages of Chopin, Liszt, and Mendelssohn.
Nocturne 14 rises to the quick
intensity that touches his Irish Dublin.

The sound of eggshells rubbing the wind.
Oysters tucked in sand give birth to pearl light.
Water dances and slips over rocks,
fresh sounds to a rare river.

A soft breeze unafraid to whisper to itself.
Amber light under cross-stitched sound.
The Kremlin's red dust hard frozen.
This cold place holds John.

AFTER HOURS

Paradise

Eruptions sloshed the corridors
of Old Main. Truth and Beauty were done
for another week. Friday, 4:15.

Delores and Julia wanted to take me to Paradise.
How do you get to Paradise? I've never been.

Take the streetcar down Woodward to Selden,
past the Graystone Ballroom, the Majestic Theatre,
the prison-flannel National Bank of Detroit, and
the orange-painted secondhand bookstore.

High-yella Delores, with garden green eyes, reached
still higher; she always seemed ready for a seance.

Julia wore her Paradise dress that grabbed her
secure all over. She didn't stop time when she walked.
She just created motion, then deep froze it.

The seams of her dress overflowed just enough to let
you know what they were holdin'. Big gams, too.

From the top balcony of Paradise,
I saw Lady Day looking for her "Lover Man,"
"Flying Home" Hampton, and Dinah
"Ain't Nobody's Business If I Do."

When I go back to Paradise (Orchestra Hall)
and hear the Guarneri Quartet or the
Detroit Symphony, I look to the top balcony.

I still hear Basie, Diz and Bird, and Mr. B's
"Cottage for Sale." Hey, you know what?
I betcha Julia is still freezin' things.

Caliban's Sonata

I am Caliban, giver of light,
puppy-headed monster, moon
calf, plain fish, natural man.

I bear wood to flame the light
for Prosper to hold the sea
and call Ariel to make music.

Art survives when pushed
and pulled. Prosper, this thing of
light, I acknowledge mine.

Fugueing Bob Kaufman

No prints, no nothing.
I walked through a house of flour
with a golden sardine in my teeth.

I danced on the wall
humming an angry love song,

shimmied through a forest of rap joints,
left prayers on a cinnamon altar
like Bird chug-a-lugging the moon,

looked to white mountains of ice
through varicose eyes of silence.

With a ditty bag full of seaweed
from the purple river, draped
in garlands of mushroom dust,

I carried fish-scales from
the orange-pekoe shore, pages

of dry-rotted time booted
from Atlantis, and felt Matisse
on the braille-white sheets.

Give me my propers.

How Would I Know?

Never thought I would know
how to talk to trees; maybe I don't,
but I'm gonna try.

I have, when no one was listening
'cept maybe that damn ol' owl
on the stump.

Even if I had the strength
to turn God inside out,
how would I know?

Seer of time, reader of leaves
and palms, tell me
what do the trees say?

Hidden in their bark and
deep roots, sometimes we are
stillborn and never know it.

I Can't Pray For You

I pray for the woman-child, seven plus seven,
who carries in her womb, a heartbeat away,
a life she must succor without understanding.

I pray for those who can't forgive,
who make no mistakes,
who have never said "I love you."

I pray for grizzly bears who would destroy
the world to save their young.

I pray for waterfalls and tiny streams
that minuet through rocks and plants,
snake dancing to white thunder.

Pray for you, my friend?
Tell me how.

The Scent of Memory

We walked Traverse Bay, kicking water
at each other, looking at a glass-bottomed sky.
Two people, in sand and water.

On the lake, the smell of dogwood scrubbed
the dew. Laughter rolled over rocks and
sand, searching for holes to push through.

Stacks of Petoskey stones, night blue
embedded in ghostly white.
Wet sand rolled off our damp skin,
brown sugar on cinnamon toast.

When you smiled, orange light flashed
against a dull gray sheet. A wisp
of burned black coffee is strong enough
to resurrect anything.

Remember

Skintight sounds
haunt the night.

As we fold ourselves
into one another,

no matter how soft
you leave,

I will think of you
and remember.

Fall Promise

The sun squats on the edge of August
and smooth orange-yellow days
seem to stop quicker than they used to.
The lukewarm October light remembers.

We watched brown leaves fling around
then stumble in their last dance.
You said, "I can't marry you now,
but don't worry. I will."

Shadows duck between window blinds
and brightness dimples the bedspread.
You will come into my arms. I will know you
again, when the sun locks eyes with the sky
and hoodwinks the heat of summer.

Academize

Standing in the courtyard of the Acropolis
with slop jars cocked at high noon,
slosh burning the soles of our naked feet,
spoon-feed we, then, each to the other, truth,
bequeathing it a rich legacy to our issue.
Only the students blinked.

Body and Soul

Coleman Hawkins recorded "Body and Soul,"
a 1939 masterpiece. My kind of jazz.

My life a wreck you're making

Everyone waited for "Body and Soul."
Time to coote across the floor,

slower than slow.

If Gwen was there, all the studs would break
into a slow trot in her direction.

I only knew how to two-step. Still do.

The only dance I ever learned. The two-step
was born for "Body and Soul."

No light could creep between dancers' bodies.

To dance with Gwen was to go places
you'd never been, softer than foam on beer.

I wonder if Gwen's still stepping.

Whatyousee

I don't wanna survive
a long slow death march,
castration by numbers,
one hair at a time.

I will not be ignored.
I'm not a secondhand pile
in the back room
of a rummage sale.

Look to the eyes of survivors,
deep sockets veiled by
flaps of skin, that once
seduced and caressed.

I do, I will shout the life out
of life—in my time, in my way.

Not by the whim of a nerve
distracted from its own reality.
Not as a cellophane package
contrived to satisfy and please.

I, Too, One Day Will Die

I, too, one day will die.
Will it be on some dark stinking street
running horizontal to the rest of the world?

For certain, no marble hall or sacred place.
Should it be in my city that I have loved
ever since I walked its summer sidewalks?

Walked rat-infested, garbage-laden alleys
that served as the playing fields of Eton,
negotiating ice when Hawk was taking names.

Maybe on the hillside where flowers, grass,
even weeds struggle for life, oversee my world,
help me remember what it was, and never was.

There will be no flashing lights, crescendo
of music: the bright sounds come when we celebrate
the living of life by living it.

POSTSCRIPT

Bobweaving: the act and action of ducking and returning punches in boxing; a way of coping and also of winning with a canny mix of humility and bravura. A fighter, "The Old Mongoose," is exemplary in the poem which shows how it's done: *Archwald Lee Wright, born age three, bobweaved himself into Archie Moore*. Bobweaving is about fighting, and not. It textures certain poems; sometimes with ambivalence, Murray suggests it might help us *celebrate the living of life by living it*.

First and foremost, Murray was a teacher. During his last illness, cards and letters came to the hospital from generations of students in virtually every walk and station of life. Messages from every student in his last class testify to the ways he was responsible to education, responsible for transforming and personalizing their—and our—education in teaching and writing or, more simply, in living and loving. Murray's poetic lessons, his *Bobweaving Detroit*, continue to teach even now.

This is the occasion to remember that Murray Jackson, educator and politician, had a public life that is encrypted, sometimes sounded, in his poems. Here, legions of friends, colleagues, but new readers as well, can hear echoes and allusions that bridge private and public in the pathos and sublimity of becoming oneself by reading deeply the recurrences of what had seemed unique. Whether referencing specific historical events and the prosaic cartography of an inner-city university, or tapping a common root of desire, Murray wrote for strangers and also for the accidental mentors, the unknown pupils who share the tender erotics of learning. One must bring to reading the knowledge of her own present moment to take away the wisdom embedded in the quick gaze as well as the studied phrase of the poetic, let alone the athletic teacher. Thus, about one of his first humanities professors as about signal black athletes, Jackson could fashion tributes that abbreviate the poet's own experience on several playing fields even as they honor the manifold and rigorous discipline necessary for intellectual, physical, and civic labor. In this way, our reading of the poems makes immediate a historical record to which one already had access, even without knowledge of the particulars. For example, Jackie Robinson put on a Brooklyn Dodger's uniform and assumed an image identified in "Pigeon-Toed Knock-Kneed": *In his private space, his blue cap over his heart, it was worth the wounds.* He (and here the pronoun names both Jackie Robinson and Murray Jackson) taught teachers how to teach; several poems, especially "First Class," suggest how much Murray Jackson took from credentialed as well as accidental professors and, in turn, what he brought to his profession.

Murray came late to recording and publishing his poetry: *Woodland Sketches: Scenes from Childhood* appeared in 1991 and *Watermelon Rinds and Cherry Pits* in 1992. It was in mourning his first wife, his older brother, his mother that he began to recollect the markers he had left on the street, on his streets peopled and shadowed with desire—his own and others'. In making us look, hear, sometimes touch, taste, and measure the reality that we are continually making and remaking, Murray invoked time and place—a layered Detroit—at once retrospective or *(past)oral* and prospective. His public readings seemed to give voice to a shared past, a life of walking the proud boulevards of a disappeared Detroit. Still, the streets he made his own offer lessons in giving and receiving hard love. Sometimes they are hard to love, but one might learn a great deal about love from *rat-infested, garbage-laden alleys that served as the playing fields of Eton.*

Evoked by the ornaments of nature, Murray's pastoral scenes were about writing, and they were deliberately written from perspectives he knew well but continued exploring. As he wondered at death or wandered in Sherwood Forest (name and neighborhood redolent of fantasies past), this poet found flowers of rhetoric to admonish those who would be merely sentimental or simply nostalgic: *Flowers, grass, even weeds help me remember what it was and never was.* In an embrace that informs and transforms, love leaks everywhere into and from these poems. Shuttling between past and future, this love gives texture to desire and remarks satisfaction and its impossibility. Death leaves promissory notes: *You will come into my arms. I will know you again.*

There was never a time when Murray Jackson was not a poet, one who makes and remarks visions. He danced among new permutations of what some would oppose or at least see in opposition: improvising and interpreting—both tensely present progressive. If his poems appear to face the past nostalgically, to return to see with fresh eyes the boyhood scenes of the mature poet, look again at the mood and tense of his verbs. The poems move, transforming time by insinuating the present into that which passes or passes most of us by as we try so hard to attain a future different from the place and way we came up. Murray was comfortable with who he was, confident that the future would grant time for becoming more himself, more ourselves. Like the *-ing* verbs that frequent them, these poems act on and in a present that is at once expectant and passing. The poet has paused looking both ways, before and after. Like the activity they record, these poems are both spontaneous and revisionary. Murray was usually out and about *in my city that I have loved since I walked its summer sidewalks.* Yet he was also reserved within himself. He sounded the depths of remembered desire in poems that echo familiar lines from blues, jazz, and the Romantic repertoire. In contradictions, Murray's poems seek to learn and teach real images that poets both improvise and interpret. Thus, "Ars Poetica" announces desiderata that entwine substance and shade: *But shadows come from real images, and I need to know the color and feel of the shadows.* Such soundings are instrumental: they are aural and mathematical; they measure and are measured. They sound the depths of remembered desires; sometimes these are invoked or provoked by tones, by favorite tunes, or by the very music of words. Just so, Murray hopes to touch not the thing itself but the shadows behind its image.

Although Murray's final illness precluded further progress on this collection after January 2001, by then he had established its basic architecture, produced a provisional table of contents, and distributed copies of the work-in-progress to his colleagues, inviting their comments while continuing to write and revise. This book is based on that manuscript.

Murray's selections tellingly favored poems that revealed his wryly compassionate engagement with the world over those of a more private or occasional provenance. These selections were drawn, with few exceptions, from his first book, *Woodland Sketches*, and from new, mostly unpublished work composed between 1993 and 2000. To these, the editors have restored a number of poems from *Watermelon Rinds and Cherry Pits* that clearly meet the standards of the book he had envisioned. As it stands, twenty-eight of the fifty-four poems included here are previously uncollected.

Murray was much given to tacitly correcting manuscript errors and omissions he discovered in the course of his public readings—and by 1998, he had begun to give increasing attention to the formal aspects of his work. As we began working together on this collection, he came to feel that the verse paragraph, on which he typically relied to produce his working drafts, was too prosaic a vehicle for the tenor of his thoughts. Editorial revisions of the individual poems were deeply informed by his desire to reshape the poems, as well as by the obligation to correct various surface errors that had appeared in his previous books.

Finally, it should be remembered that Murray's abiding love of the vernacular was of a piece with his love of classic literature. Though he came rather late to the practice of poetry, and had already "worn a few hats" in his time, he counted his membership in the community of poets as an essential element in his legacy.

Ted Pearson
Kathryne V. Lindberg

Murray Earl Jackson

Murray Jackson was born December 21, 1926, in Philadelphia. His family moved to Detroit in 1929, where, though traveling widely, he continued to live and work until his death on February 5, 2002. He attended Detroit public schools, graduating from Northern High School in 1944. At Northern, he was a member of the football, tennis, and track teams as well as a lieutenant in the ROTC. After graduation, during World War II, he served as a Chief Petty Officer in the Navy. Stationed near San Diego, he taught physical fitness and conditioning courses while continuing his own athletic training. Following his discharge, Jackson returned to Detroit to begin a career in education and community leadership. Although offered a contract with the Brooklyn Dodgers (within a year of Jackie Robinson's ascension to the Majors), Jackson chose to attend Wayne State University on the GI Bill. At Wayne, and briefly at Adrian College (1950), he pursued his twin passions for athletics and Classical scholarship, focusing on Roman history and Greek literature. He received bachelor's (1954) and master's degrees (1956) from the Humanities Department at Wayne State. While a student, he also worked at Wayne State as an academic counselor and for the Detroit Youth Home as a group counselor.

As he was to do throughout his adult life, Jackson also served informally as an intellectual coach and civic example; his younger contemporaries remember still this star athlete, "race man," and player at his "main job" of mentoring youngsters in public schools and at community gyms. In the late 1950s and 1960s, Murray served Wayne State as assistant dean of students, and as assistant to the vice president for urban affairs. In 1980, he was elected to the first of three eight-year terms as a member of the Board of Governors at Wayne State University. In these capacities, Jackson worked directly to open the university to the community and cultural life of Detroit. He enabled countless youngsters to believe in themselves and to march, often behind the back of Jim Crow, into the university—and from there to lead full and professionally rewarding lives. Jackson himself was deliberate in living ethically and aesthetically to achieve a personable mixture of gravitas and humor: yes, he really did hold informal seminars in art history at the Hazel Park racetrack.

From 1965 to 1969, Jackson chaired Michigan's first district of the Democratic party He was also a consultant and member of the Democratic party's Education Committee, the Citizens Advisory Committee to the Detroit Public Schools, and the Michigan House of Representative's Committee on Colleges and Universities. In 1964, he and his first wife Dauris (1932–1979), herself a distinguished educator, writer, and public servant, were the first African Americans (post-Reconstruction) to be seated at a Michigan Democratic Convention. After working to elect Detroit's first black mayor, state senator Coleman A. Young, Jackson served on the Advisory Committee for the Mayor of Detroit, the Mayor's Committee for the Rehabilitation of Narcotic Addicts, the Senior Citizens Commission, and the Southeast Michigan Transportation Authority. In 1975, he became the first executive director of the Detroit Council of the Arts, where he spearheaded a city proposal to require developers to devote a minimum of 1.5 percent of their building costs to aesthetics and systematic urban beautification.

From the 1970s through the 1990s, Jackson, who earned two doctorates, *Honoris Causa*, in the humanities—from Shaw College (1970) and from Wayne State University (2001)—served with distinction on more boards and commissions than his humility would permit him to enumerate. A partial inventory would reveal that while teaching full-time at the University of Michigan, Jackson was president of the American Lung Association of Southeastern Michigan, and was on the boards of directors for the Neighborhood Service Organization, Big

Brothers and Sisters of America, the Detroit Council for Youth Services, the Michigan Women's Studies Association, the Council on Black American Affairs of the Association of Community and Junior Colleges, and Wayne State's Higher Education Opportunity Committee.

He more recently served on the boards of Michigan Prospects for Renewed Citizenship, a progressive advocacy PAC; the Detroit-Livernois Co-operative Association; Mariners Inn and Jefferson House, two substance-abuse rehabilitation centers; the Student Advocacy Center, which keeps children in school and out of the criminal justice system; and Inside/Out, a program that brings professional writers together with middle- and high-school artists and writers. He was also long-term or life member of the NAACP, the Urban League, and the American Association of University Professors.

Murray was always prepared to teach by precept, but also by example: in high school, he was among the youngest black men to become an Eagle Scout; and as a Wayne State alumnus, he rose to grand pole-march of the Detroit Alumni Chapter of Kappa Alpha Psi, and he received the Elder W. Diggs Award of the Grand Chapter of the Fraternity. *But* none of these honors and commitments prevented Jackson from regular attendance at a poker game that convened regularly for some forty years of Friday nights.

In 1970, Jackson became the founding president of Wayne County Community College, an institution whose establishment and growth was at first resisted by a hostile white establishment; despite enrollments of over twenty thousand, it did not gain municipal millage until the 1990s. In 1972, he joined the University of Michigan at Ann Arbor as a tenured professor in the Center for the Study of Higher Education. The generations of teachers whom he taught—and several published essays that are at once academically sound and polemical in their advocacy—attest to Jackson's career-long commitment to urban higher education. In the 1980s, as a lecturer and consultant, he traveled to Africa,

China, and throughout the United States. He continued to serve as a mentor, instructor, and administrator of urban higher education until his formal retirement in 1992.

Jackson then resumed his public life in the humanities by teaching at least one university course and several workshops a year. He read his poetry at numerous venues in Michigan, at Chicago's Harold Washington Library, Dartmouth College, Washington State University, and many other colleges in Connecticut, Nebraska, Massachusetts, Maine, Wisconsin, and, in 1994, at the Dartington International Literature Festival in England. He also conducted workshops at the YWCA, the Detroit Public Library, and at several public schools and nursing homes. Whether at such venues, or in "Poetry and the City, From Augustine to St. Antoine Street" in Ann Arbor's Freshman Seminar Program, or in seminars, including "Poetry and Urban Life" at Wayne State, Jackson wove the texts of poetry and Detroit together for all manner of students.

After the fall semester of 1999, illness prevented him from personally teaching his varied publics. Until his death, he and Professor Kathryne V. Lindberg, who married in 1994, lived in downtown Detroit. Dr. Jackson is survived by his daughter, Llenda Jackson-Leslie, who is a writer and political consultant, his son, M. David Jackson, MD, three grandsons, Christopher, Eric, Gregory, and his younger brother and lifelong friend, Lawrence Jackson, MD. In December 2001, to recognize his dedication, love, and service to his community and university, the Board of Governors of Wayne State University presented Murray Jackson an Honorary Doctorate of Humane Letters and appointed him governor emeritus. The board further honored him by establishing a scholarship in his name. This book and its proceeds are dedicated to the Murray Jackson Fellowship for Master's Students in the Humanities.